T5-ARK-519

Ven. Francisco Marto
Of Fatima

*"Thou hast taught me, O God,
from my youth."*

—Psalm 70:17

OTHER BOOKLETS
BY THE SAME AUTHOR

The Rosary and the Crisis of Faith

The Forgotten Secret of Fatima

St. Joseph, Fatima and Fatherhood

Fatima's Message for Our Times

I Wait For You (Editor)

Ven. Jacinta Marto of Fatima

Ven. Francisco Marto Of Fatima

Compiled by

Msgr. Joseph A. Cirrincione
(From *Fatima, In Lucia's Own Words*)

"And I looked for one that would grieve together with me, but there was none: and for one that would comfort me, and I found none."
—Psalm 68:21

TAN BOOKS AND PUBLISHERS, INC.
Rockford, Illinois 61105

The Introduction to this booklet copyright © 1994 by TAN Books and Publishers, Inc. The body of this booklet is excerpted from *Fatima, In Lucia's Own Words*, by permission of the Carmel of Coimbra and of Father Louis Kondor, SVD, Vice-Postulator of the Cause for Jacinta and Francisco Marto.

Library of Congress Catalog Card No.: 94-61207

ISBN: 0-89555-511-5

Printed and bound in the United States of America.

The type in this book is the property of TAN Books and Publishers, Inc., and may not be reproduced, in whole or in part, without written permission of the Publisher.

TAN BOOKS AND PUBLISHERS, INC.
P.O. Box 424
Rockford, Illinois 61105

1994

"At that hour the disciples came to Jesus, saying: Who thinkest thou is the greater in the kingdom of heaven? And Jesus calling unto him a little child, set him in the midst of them, and said: Amen I say to you, unless you be converted, and become as little children, you shall not enter into the kingdom of heaven. Whosoever therefore shall humble himself as this little child, he is the greater in the kingdom of heaven."

—*Matthew* 18:1-4

CONTENTS

INTRODUCTION

Earlier this year (1994) as the 60th Anniversary of my priestly Ordination began to draw near (June 9), I began to feel a desire to observe it at the Shrine of Our Lady of Fatima in Portugal, if it was God's will. "If it was God's will" meant if everything fell into place that had to fall into place for me to go. At 84, one does not contemplate so strenuous a journey without qualms. First, I would take it as a favorable sign if plane space were available on the days I had in mind. Also, a room in my favorite hotel in Fatima had to be available.

But, most of all, my doctor had to assure me that I could stand the strain of a transatlantic flight with its normal attendant problems.

When I received my doctor's consent and approval for the trip, I took it as a sign that it was God's will that I should go to Fatima to observe there my 60th ordination anniversary.

I had another reason for wanting to go to Fatima. I wanted to correct in print a wrong impression I had unintentionally given of Venerable Francisco in a pamphlet I had written about Venerable Jacinta Marto two years previously. In consulting books on Fatima written before the publication of *Fatima, In Lucia's Own Words* I copied a version of the dialogue between Our Lady and Lucia that went as follows:

"Fear not," the Lady said, "I will not harm you."

"Where are you from?" Lucia asked.

"I am from Heaven," the beautiful Lady replied.

"What do you want of me?" Lucia asked.

"I come to ask you to come here for six consecutive months, on the thirteenth day, at this same hour. I will tell you later who I am and what I want."

"Am I going to Heaven?" Lucia asked.

"Yes, you shall," the Lady assured her.

"And Jacinta?"

"Yes."

"And Francisco?"

"He too shall go, but he must say many Rosaries."

In quoting the dialogue in the pamphlet on Jacinta, I wrote that Our Lady said regarding Francisco, "He will go also, but *first* he must recite many Rosaries." In her fourth memoir, Lucia quotes Our Lady as saying: "Yes, he shall go, but he must say many Rosaries." She did not say "But *FIRST* he must say many Rosaries."

This puts an entirely different complexion on

the matter. Our Lady did not add a condition to Francisco's going to Heaven. She was not implying the existence of a defect in Francisco that would keep him from going to Heaven. My interpretation of the dialogue now is: Our Lady was simply declaring Francisco's mission. It would be the frequent recitation of the Rosary.

Incidentally, during the apparition, Francisco did not see the Lady nor hear her speak, though he could hear Lucia talking. When Lucia brought this to Our Lady's attention, she replied: "Let him say the Rosary and he too will see me."

Happy at Our Lady's promise that he would go to Heaven, Francisco exclaimed: "Oh, my dear Lady! I'll say as many Rosaries as you want." Later we will see how faithful the little boy was to that promise.

Thus I had two reasons for going to Fatima: in thanksgiving for my 60 years of priesthood and to obtain permission to use Sister Lucia's Memoirs in writing a booklet on Venerable Francisco.

Fatima, In Lucia's Own Words was published by Father Louis Kondor, SVD, Vice-Postulator of the cause for the beatifications of Venerable Francisco and Venerable Jacinta Marto. The Postulation Centre in Fatima which he heads has the rights to *Fatima, In Lucia's Own Words*.

Thus I needed not only Sister Lucia's permission, but Father Kondor's as well.

Before I left for Fatima, I wrote to Mother Prioress of the Coimbra Carmelite Community, of which Sister Lucia is a member, to tell her of my pilgrimage to Fatima and of my intention to pay her a visit while there. She replied by extending an invitation to visit the Convent and promised prayers for a safe trip.

While in Fatima, I paid a visit first to the Monastery Pius XII, a community of English-speaking cloistered Dominican nuns where I had been a guest many times before in their chaplain's quarters. They offered to keep in touch with Mother Prioress in Coimbra and let me know what day would be best for a visit to Coimbra.

Divine Providence, which had smiled so graciously on my pilgrimage thus far, continued to do so, for the day settled on for my trip to Coimbra was June 16, the very day the Dominican Sisters were to celebrate the 40th Anniversary of their foundation in Fatima. Father Kondor and the retired Bishop of Fatima-Leiria were both to be present for the occasion. I was invited as well, but had to pass it up because a flare-up of a chronic bronchial condition made it imprudent to attend the anniversary celebration and to travel to Coimbra on the same day.

I hired a car and driver for the hour's ride to Coimbra and reached there at the appointed time.

The visit with the Carmelite Community went very well, and I was more than repaid for my pains by receiving the permission I desired from both the Coimbra Carmel and Father Kondor, who was contacted while still at Fatima.

Which finally brings us to the story of *Ven. Francisco Marto Of Fatima,* as told by Sister Lucia in *Fatima, In Lucia's Own Words.*

Msgr. Joseph A. Cirrincione
Feast of Our Lady of Mt. Carmel
July 16, 1994

Ven. Francisco Marto
Of Fatima

FRANCISCO'S CHARACTER
(From *Fatima, In Lucia's Own Words*)

FRANCISCO'S SPIRITUALITY

I am going to begin then, Your Excellency, by writing what God wills to bring to my mind about Francisco. I hope that Our Lord will make him know in Heaven what I am writing about him on earth, so that he may intercede for me with Jesus and Mary, especially during these coming days.

The affection which bound me to Francisco was just one of kinship, and one which had its origin in the graces which Heaven deigned to grant us.

Apart from his features and his practice of virtue, Francisco did not seem at all to be Jacinta's brother. Unlike her, he was neither capricious nor vivacious. On the contrary, he was quiet and submissive by nature.

When we were at play and he won the game, if anyone made a point of denying him his rights as winner, he yielded without more ado and merely said: "You think you won? That's all right! I don't mind!"

He showed no love for dancing, as Jacinta

1

did; he much preferred playing the flute while the others danced.

In our games he was quite lively; but few of us liked to play with him, as he nearly always lost. I must confess that I myself did not always feel too kindly disposed towards him, as his naturally calm temperament exasperated my own excessive vivacity. Sometimes I caught him by the arm, made him sit down on the ground or on a stone, and told him to keep still; he obeyed me as if I had real authority over him. Afterwards, I felt sorry and went and took him by the hand, and he would come along with me as good-humoredly as though nothing had happened. If one of the other children insisted on taking away something belonging to him, he said: "Let them have it! What do I care?"

I recall how, one day, he came to my house and was delighted to show me a handkerchief with a picture of Our Lady of Nazaré on it, which someone had brought him from the seaside. All the children gathered round him to admire it. The handkerchief was passed from hand to hand, and in a few minutes it disappeared. We looked for it, but it was nowhere to be found. A little later, I found it myself in another small boy's pocket. I wanted to take it away from him, but he insisted that it was his own and that someone had brought him one from the beach as well. To put an end to the quarrel, Francisco then went up to him and said: "Let him have it! What does a handkerchief matter to me?" My own opinion is that, if he had lived to manhood, his greatest defect would have been his attitude of "never mind!"

When I was seven and began to take our sheep out to pasture, he seemed to be quite indifferent. In the evenings, he waited for me in my parents' yard with his little sister, but this was not out of affection for me, but rather to please her. As soon as Jacinta heard the tinkling of the sheep bells, she ran out to meet me; whereas, Francisco waited for me, sitting on the stone steps leading up to our front door. Afterwards, he came with us to play on the old threshing floor, while we watched for Our Lady and the Angels to light their lamps [the stars]. He eagerly counted the stars with us, but nothing enchanted him as much as the beauty of sunrise or sunset. As long as he could still glimpse one last ray of the setting sun, he made no attempt to watch for the first lamp to be lit in the sky.

"No lamp is as beautiful as Our Lord's," he used to remark to Jacinta, who much preferred Our Lady's lamp because, as she explained, "It doesn't hurt our eyes." Enraptured, he watched the sunrays glinting on the window panes of the homes in the neighboring villages, or glistening in the drops of water which spangled the trees and furze bushes of the serra, making them shine like so many stars; in his eyes these were a thousand times more beautiful than the Angels' lamps.

When he persisted in pleading with his mother to let him take care of the flock and therefore come along with me, it was more to please Jacinta than anything else, for she much preferred Francisco's company to that of her brother John. One day his mother, already quite annoyed, refused this permission, and he answered with his usual tranquility: "Mother, it doesn't matter to me. It's Jacinta who wants me to go." He confirmed this on yet another occasion. One of my companions came to my house to invite me to go with her, as she had a particularly good pasturage in view for that day. As the sky was overcast, I went to my aunt's house to inquire who was going out that day, Francisco and Jacinta, or their brother John; in case of the latter, I preferred the company of my former companion. My aunt had already decided that, as it looked like rain, John should go. But Francisco went to his mother again, and insisted on going himself. He received a curt and decided "No," whereupon he exclaimed:

"It's all the same with me. It is Jacinta who feels badly about it."

NATURAL INCLINATIONS

What Francisco enjoyed most, when we were out on the mountains together, was to perch on

4

the top of the highest rock, and sing or play his flute. If his little sister came down to run races with me, he stayed up there entertaining himself with his music and song.

He always took part in our games when we invited him, but he seldom waxed enthusiastic, remarking: "I'll go, but I know I'll be the loser." These were the games we knew and found most entertaining: pebbles, forfeits, pass the ring, buttons, hit the mark, quoits, and card games such as the bisca game, turning up the kings, queens and knaves, and so on. We had two packs of cards; I had one and they had the other. Francisco liked best to play cards, and the bisca was his favorite game.

FRANCISCO SEES THE ANGEL

During the Apparition of the Angel, he prostrated like his sister and myself, carried away by the same supernatural force that moved us to do so; but he learned the prayer by hearing us repeat it, since, he told us, he heard nothing of what the Angel said.

Afterwards, when we prostrated to say that prayer, he was the first to feel the strain of such a posture; but he remained kneeling or sitting, and still praying until we had finished. Later he said: "I am not able to stay like that for a long time, like you. My back aches so much that I can't do it."

At the second Apparition of the Angel, down

by the well, Francisco waited a few moments after it was over, then asked:

"You spoke to the Angel. What did he say to you?"

"Didn't you hear?"

"No. I could see that he was talking to you. I heard what you said to him; but what he said to you, I don't know."

As the supernatural atmosphere in which the Angel left us, had not yet entirely disappeared, I told him to ask Jacinta or myself next day.

"Jacinta, you tell me what the Angel said."

"I'll tell you tomorrow. Today I can't talk about it."

Next day, as soon as he came up to me, he asked me:

"Did you sleep last night? I kept thinking about the Angel, and what he could have said."

I then told him all that the Angel had said at the first and second Apparitions. But it seemed that he had not received an understanding of all that the words meant, for he asked:

"Who is the Most High? What is the meaning of 'The Hearts of Jesus and Mary are attentive to the voice of your supplications?'. . ."

Having received an answer, he remained deep in thought for a while and then broke in with another question. But my mind was not yet free, so I told him to wait until the next day because at that moment I was unable to speak. He waited quite contentedly, but he did not let slip the very next opportunity of putting more questions. This made Jacinta say to him:

"Listen! We shouldn't talk much about these things."

When we spoke about the Angel, I don't know what it was that we felt.

"I don't know how I feel," Jacinta said. "I can no longer talk or sing or play. I haven't strength enough for anything."

"Neither have I," replied Francisco, "but what of it? The Angel is more beautiful than all this. Let's think about him."

In the third Apparition, the presence of the supernatural made itself felt more intensely still. For several days even Francisco did not venture to speak. Later he said:

"I love to see the Angel, but the worst of it is that, afterwards, we are unable to do anything. I couldn't even walk. I don't know what was the matter with me."

In spite of that, after the third Apparition of the Angel, it was he who noticed that it was getting dark and who drew our attention to the fact and thought we should take our flocks back home.

Once the first few days were over and we had returned to normal, Francisco asked:

"The Angel gave you Holy Communion, but what was it that he gave to Jacinta and me?"

"It was Holy Communion, too," replied Jacinta, with inexpressible joy. "Didn't you see

7

that it was the Blood that fell from the Host?"

"I felt that God was within me, but I did not know how!"

Then, prostrating on the ground, he and his sister remained for a long time, saying over and over again the prayer of the Angel, "Most Holy Trinity. . ."

Little by little, the atmosphere of the supernatural faded away, and by the 13th of May, we were playing with almost as much enjoyment and freedom of spirit as we had done before.

IMPRESSIONS OF THE FIRST APPARITION

The Apparition of Our Lady plunged us once more into the atmosphere of the supernatural, but this time more gently. Instead of that annihilation in the Divine Presence, which exhausted us even physically, it left us filled with peace and expansive joy, which did not prevent us from speaking afterwards of what had happened. However, with regard to the light communicated to us when Our Lady opened her hands and everything connected with this light, we experienced a kind of interior impulse that compelled us to keep silent.

Afterwards, we told Francisco all that Our Lady had said. He was overjoyed and expressed the happiness he felt when he heard of the promise that he would go to Heaven. Crossing his hands on his breast, he exclaimed, "Oh, my dear Our Lady! I'll say as many rosaries as you want!" And from then on, he made a habit of moving away from us, as though going for a walk. When we called him and asked him what he was doing, he raised his hand and showed me his rosary. If we told him to come and play, and say the Rosary with us afterwards, he replied:

"I'll pray then as well. Don't you remember that Our Lady said I must pray many Rosaries?"

He said to me on one occasion: "I loved seeing the Angel, but I loved still more seeing Our Lady. What I loved most of all was to see Our Lord in that light from Our Lady which penetrated our hearts. I love God so much! But He is very sad because of so many sins! We must never commit any sins again."

I have already said, in the second account about Jacinta, how he was the one who gave me the news that she had broken our agreement not to say anything. As he shared my opinion that the matter should be kept secret, he added sadly: "As for me, when my mother asked me if it were true, I had to say that it was, so as not to tell a lie."

From time to time, he said: "Our Lady told us that we would have much to suffer, but I don't mind. I'll suffer all that she wishes! What I want is to go to Heaven!"

One day, when I showed how unhappy I was over the persecution now beginning both in my family and outside, Francisco tried to encourage me with these words:

"Never mind! Didn't Our Lady say that we would have much to suffer, to make reparation to Our Lord and to her own Immaculate Heart for all the sins by which They are offended? They are so sad! If we can console Them with these sufferings, how happy we shall be!"

When we arrived at our pasturage a few days after Our Lady's first Apparition, he climbed up to the top of a steep rock, and called out to us:

"Don't come up here; let me stay here alone."

"All right." And off I went, chasing butterflies with Jacinta. We no sooner caught them than we made the sacrifice of letting them fly away, and we never gave another thought to Francisco. When lunch time came, we missed him and went to call him:

"Francisco, don't you want to come for your lunch?"

"No, you eat."

"And to pray the Rosary?"

"That, yes, later on. Call me again."

When I went to call him again, he said to me:

"You come up here and pray with me."

We climbed up to the peak, where the three of us could scarcely find room to kneel down, and I asked him:

"But what have you been doing all this time?"

"I am thinking about God, Who is so sad because of so many sins! If only I could give Him joy!"

One day, we began to sing in happy chorus about the joys of the serra.

We sang it right through once and were about to repeat it, when Francisco interrupted us: "Let's not sing anymore. Since we saw the Angel and Our Lady, singing doesn't appeal to me any longer."

IMPRESSIONS OF THE SECOND APPARITION

At the second Apparition on June 13th, 1917, Francisco was deeply impressed by the light which, as I related in the second account, Our Lady communicated to us at the moment when she said: "My Immaculate Heart will be your refuge and the way which will lead you to God." At the time, he did not seem to grasp the significance of what was happening, perhaps because it was not given to him to hear the accompanying words. For this reason, he asked later:

"Why did Our Lady have a Heart in her hand, spreading out over the world that great light which is God? You were with Our Lady in the light which went down towards the earth, and Jacinta was with me in the light which rose towards Heaven!"

"That is because you and Jacinta will soon go to Heaven," I replied, "while I, with the Immaculate Heart of Mary, will remain for some time longer on earth."

"How many years longer will you stay here?" he asked.

"I don't know. Quite a lot."

"Was it Our Lady who said so?"

"Yes, and I saw it in the light that she shone into our hearts."

Jacinta confirmed the very same thing, saying:

"It is just like that! That's exactly how I saw it too!"

He remarked sometimes:

"These people are so happy just because you told them that Our Lady wants the Rosary said, and that you are to learn to read! How would they feel if they only knew what she showed to us in God, in her Immaculate Heart, in that great light! But this is a secret; it must not be spoken about. It's better that no one should know it."

After this Apparition, whenever they asked us if Our Lady had said anything else, we began to give this reply: "Yes, she did, but it's a secret." If they asked us why it was a secret, we shrugged our shoulders, lowered our heads and kept silent. But, after the 13th of July, we said: "Our Lady told us we were not to tell it to anybody," thus referring to the secret imposed on us by Our Lady.

FRANCISCO STRENGTHENS LUCIA'S COURAGE

In the course of this month, the influx of people increased considerably, and so did the constant questionings and contradictions. Francisco suffered quite a lot from all this and complained to his sister, saying:

"What a pity! If you'd only kept quiet, no one would know! If only it were not a lie, we could tell all the people that we saw nothing, and that would be the end of it. But this can't be done!"

When he saw me perplexed and in doubt, he wept and said:

"But how can you think that it is the devil? Didn't you see Our Lady and God in that great light? How can we go there without you, when it is you who do the talking?"

That night after supper he came back to my house, called me out to the old threshing floor and said:

"Look! Aren't you going tomorrow?"

"I'm not going. I've already told you I'm not going back there any more."

"But what a shame! Why is it that you now think that way? Don't you see that it can't be the devil? God is already sad enough on account of so many sins, and now if you don't go, He'll be sadder still! Come on, say you'll go!"

"I've already told you I'm not going. It's no use asking me." And I returned abruptly to the house.

A few days later, he said to me: "You know, I never slept at all that night. I spent the whole time crying and praying, begging Our Lady to make you go!"

IMPRESSIONS OF THE THIRD APPARITION

In the third Apparition, Francisco seemed to be the one on whom the vision of Hell made the least impression, though it did indeed have quite a considerable effect on him. What made the most powerful impression on him and what wholly absorbed him, was God, the Most Holy Trinity, perceived in that light which penetrated our inmost souls. Afterwards, he said:

"We were on fire in that light which is God, and yet we were not burnt! What is God?. . .We could never put it into words. Yes, that is something indeed which we could never express! But what a pity it is that He is so sad! If only I could console Him!. . ."

One day, I was asked if Our Lady had told us to pray for sinners, and I said she had not. At the first opportunity, while the people were questioning Jacinta, he called me aside and said:

"You lied just now! How could you say that Our Lady didn't tell us to pray for sinners? Didn't she ask us to pray for sinners, then?"

"For sinners, no! She told us to pray for peace, for the war to end. But for sinners, she told us to make sacrifices."

"Ah! That's true. I was beginning to think you had lied."

FRANCISCO IN PRISON

I have already described how Francisco spent the day praying and weeping, perhaps even more upset than I was, when my father received an order to present me before the Administrator at Vila Nova de Ourém. In prison, he was quite courageous and tried to cheer up Jacinta when she felt most homesick. While we were saying the Rosary in prison, he noticed that one of the prisoners was on his knees with his cap still on his head. Francisco went up to him and said: "If you wish to pray, you should take your cap off." Right away, the poor man handed it to him and he went over and put it on the bench on top of his own.

During Jacinta's interrogation, he confided to me with boundless joy and peace: "If they kill us as they say, we'll soon be in Heaven! How wonderful! Nothing else matters!" Then after a moment's silence, he added: "God grant that Jacinta won't be afraid. I'm going to say a Hail Mary for her!" He promptly removed his cap and prayed. The guard, seeing him praying, asked him:

"What are you saying?"

"I'm saying a Hail Mary so that Jacinta won't be afraid."

The guard made a scornful gesture and let him go ahead.

One day, after our return from Vila Nova de

Ourém, we began to be aware of the presence of the supernatural all around us and to feel that we were about to receive some heavenly communication. Francisco at once showed his concern over Jacinta's absence.

"What a pity it would be," he exclaimed, "if Jacinta did not get here in time!"

He begged his brother to go quickly and get her, adding:

"Tell her to run here."

After his brother had left us, Francisco said:

"Jacinta will be very sad if she doesn't arrive in time."

After the Apparition, his sister wanted to stay there the whole afternoon, so he said: "No! You must go home, because Mother didn't let you come out with the sheep." And to encourage her, he went back to the house with her.

In prison, when we noticed that it was already past midday and that they would not let us go to the Cova da Iria, Francisco said:

"Perhaps Our Lady will come and appear to us here."

On the following day, he could not hide his distress, and almost in tears, he said:

"Our Lady must have been very sad because we didn't go to the Cova da Iria, and she won't appear to us again, I would so love to see her!"

While in prison, Jacinta wept bitterly, for she was so homesick for her mother and all the family. Francisco tried to cheer her, saying:

"Even if we never see our mother again, let's be patient! We can offer it for the conversion of sinners. The worst thing would be if Our Lady never came back again! That is what hurts me most. But I offer this as well for sinners."

Afterwards, he asked me:

"Tell me! Will Our Lady not come and appear to us any more?"

"I don't know. I think she will."

"I miss her so much!"

The Apparition at Valinhos was, therefore, a double joy for him. He had been tormented by the fear that she would never return. He told me later:

"Most likely, she didn't appear on the 13th, so as to avoid going to the Administrator's house, maybe because he is such a bad man."

IMPRESSIONS OF THE LAST APPARITIONS

After the 13th of September, when I told Francisco that in October Our Lord would come as well, he was overwhelmed with joy. "Oh, how good He is! I've only seen Him twice, and I love Him so much!" From time to time, he asked:

"Are there many days left till the 13th? I'm longing for that day to come, so that I can see Our Lord again." Then he thought for a moment, and added:

"But listen! Will He still be so sad? I am so sorry to see Him sad like that! I offer Him all

17

the sacrifices I can think of. Sometimes, I don't even run away from all those people, just in order to make sacrifices!"

After October 13th, he said to me:

"I loved seeing Our Lord, but I loved still more seeing Him in that light where we were with Him as well. It's not long now, and Our Lord will take me up close to Him, and then I can look at Him forever."

One day, I asked him:

"When you are questioned, why do you put your head down and not want to answer?"

"Because I want you to answer, and Jacinta too. I didn't hear anything. I can only say that I saw. Then, supposing I said something you don't want me to say?"

Every now and then, he went off and left us without warning. When we missed him, we went in search of him, calling out his name. He answered from behind a little wall, or a shrub or a clump of brambles, and there he was on his knees, praying.

"Why didn't you tell us so that we could come and pray with you?"

"Because I prefer to pray alone."

[In my notes on the booklet called *Venerable Jacinta Marto of Fatima* I've already related what happened on a piece of land known as Varzea. I don't think I need to repeat it here.
—Msgr. Cirrincione.]

On our way to my home one day, we had to

pass by my godmother's house. She had just been making a mead drink and called us in to give us a glass. We went in, and Francisco was the first to whom she offered a glassful. He took it, and without drinking it, he passed it on to Jacinta, so that she and I could have a drink first. Meanwhile, he turned on his heel and disappeared.

"Where is Francisco?" my godmother asked.

"I don't know! He was here just now."

He did not return, so Jacinta and I thanked my godmother for the drink and went in search of Francisco. We knew beyond a shadow of a doubt that he would be sitting on the edge of the well which I have mentioned so often.

"Francisco, you didn't drink your glass of mead! My godmother called you so many times, and you didn't appear!"

"When I took the glass, I suddenly remembered I could offer that sacrifice to console Our Lord, so while you two were taking a drink, I ran over here."

ANECDOTES AND POPULAR SONGS

Between my house and Francisco's lived my godfather Anastacio, who was married to an older woman whom God had not blessed with children. They were farmers and quite well-off, so they didn't need to work. My father was overseer of their farm and had charge of the day laborers. In gratitude for this, they showed a special liking for me, particularly my godfather's wife, whom I called my godmother Teresa. If I didn't call in during the day, I had to go and sleep there at night, because she couldn't get along without her little "sweetmeat," as she called me.

On festive occasions, she delighted in dressing me up with her gold necklace and heavy earrings, which hung down below my shoulders, and a pretty little hat decorated with immense feathers of different colors and fastened with an array of gold beads. At the "festas," there was no one better turned out than I, and how my sisters and my godmother gloried in the fact! The other children crowded round me to admire the brilliance of my finery. To tell the truth, I myself greatly enjoyed the "festa," and vanity was my worst adornment. Everybody showed [a] liking and esteem for me, except a poor orphan girl whom my godmother Teresa had taken into her home on the death of her mother. She seemed to fear that I would get part of the inheritance she was hoping for, and indeed she would not have been mistaken, had not Our Lord destined for me a far more precious inheritance.

As soon as the news of the Apparitions got around, my godfather showed unconcern, and my godmother was completely opposed to it all. She made no secret of her disapproval of such "inventions," as she called them. I began, therefore, to keep away from her house as much as

I could. My disappearance was soon followed by that of the groups of children who so often gathered there, and whom my godmother loved to watch singing and dancing. She treated them to dried figs, nuts, almonds, chestnuts, fruit, and so on.

One Sunday afternoon, I was passing near her house with Francisco and Jacinta, when she called out to us: "Come in, my little swindlers, come! You've not been here for a long time!" Once inside, she lavished her usual attentions on us. The other children seemed to guess we were there, and began to come along as well. My kind godmother, happy at seeing us all gathered in her house once again after such a long space of time, heaped delicacies upon us and wanted to see us sing and dance.

"Come on," we said, "what will it be, this one or that?"

My godmother made the choice herself. It was "Congratulations without Illusions," a part song for boys and girls.

FRANCISCO, THE LITTLE MORALIST

The women of the neighborhood no sooner heard the lively singing than they came over to join us, and at the end they asked us to sing it through again. Francisco, however, came up to me and said: "Let's not sing that song any more. Our Lord certainly does not want us to sing things like that now." We therefore slipped away among the other children, and ran off to our favorite well.

To tell the truth, now that I have just finished writing out the song under obedience, I cover my face with shame. But Your Excellency, at the request of Rev. Dr. Galamba, has seen fit to order me to write down the popular songs that we knew. Here they are then! I do not know why they are wanted, but for me it is enough to know that I am thus fulfilling God's will.

Meanwhile, it was getting near Carnival time, in 1918. The boys and girls met once again that year to prepare the usual festive meals and fun of those days. Each one brought something from home—such as olive oil, flour, meat, and so on—to one of the houses, and the girls then did the cooking for a sumptuous banquet. All those three days, feasting and dancing went on well into the night, above all on the last day of the Carnival.

The children under fourteen had their own celebration in another house. Several of the girls came to ask me to help them organize our "festa." At first, I refused. But finally, I gave in like a coward, especially after hearing the pleading of José Carreira's sons and daughter, for it was he who had placed his home in Casa Velha at our disposal. He and his wife insistently asked me to go there. I yielded then, and went with a crowd of youngsters to see the place. There was a fine large room, almost as big as a hall, which was well suited for the amusements, and a spacious yard for the supper! Everything was arranged, and I came home, outwardly in a most festive mood, but inwardly with my conscience protesting loudly. As soon as I met Jacinta and Francisco, I told them what had happened.

"Are you going back again to those parties and games?" Francisco asked me sternly. "Have you already forgotten that we promised never to do that anymore?"

"I didn't want to go at all. But you can see how they never stopped begging me to go, and now I don't know what to do!"

There was indeed no end to the entreaties, nor to the number of girls who came insisting that I play with them. Some even came from far distant villages—from Moita came Rosa, Ana Caetano and Ana Brogueira; from Fatima, the two daughters of Manuel da Ramira, and two of Joaquim Chapeleta as well; from Amoreira, the two Silva girls; from Currais, Laura Gato, Josefa Valinho and several others whose names I have forgotten, besides those who came from Boleiros and Lomba de Pederneira, and so on; and this quite apart from all those who came from Eira da Pedra, Casa Velha and Aljustrel. How could I so suddenly let down all those girls, who seemed not to know how to enjoy themselves without my company, and make them understand that I had to stop going to

23

these gatherings once and for all? God inspired Francisco with the answer:

"Do you know how you could do it? Everybody knows that Our Lady has appeared to you. Therefore, you can say that you have promised her not to dance anymore, and for this reason you are not going! Then, on such days, we can run away and hide in the cave on the Cabeço. Up there nobody will find us!"

I accepted his proposal, and once I had made my decision, nobody else thought of organizing any such gathering. God's blessing was with us. Those friends of mine, who until then sought me out to have me join in their amusements, now followed my example, and came to my home on Sunday afternoons to ask me to go with them to pray the Rosary in the Cova da Iria.

FRANCISCO, LOVER OF SOLITUDE AND PRAYER

Francisco was a boy of few words. Whenever he prayed or offered sacrifices, he preferred to go apart and hide, even from Jacinta and myself. Quite often, we surprised him hidden behind a wall or a clump of blackberry bushes, whither he had ingeniously slipped away to kneel and pray, or "think," as he said, "of Our Lord, Who is sad on account of so many sins."

If I asked him: "Francisco, why don't you tell me to pray with you, and Jacinta too?"

"I prefer praying by myself," he answered, "so that I can think and console Our Lord, Who is so sad!"

I asked him one day:

"Francisco, which do you like better—to console Our Lord, or to convert sinners, so that no more souls will go to Hell?"

"I would rather console Our Lord. Didn't you notice how sad Our Lady was that last month, when she said that people must not offend Our Lord anymore, for He is already much offended? I would like to console Our Lord, and after that, convert sinners so that they won't offend Him anymore."

Sometimes, on our way to school, as soon as we reached Fatima, he would say to me:

"Listen! You go to school, and I'll stay here in the church, close to the Hidden Jesus. It's not worth my while learning to read, as I'll be going to Heaven very soon. On your way home, come here and call me."

The Blessed Sacrament was kept at that time near the entrance of the church, on the left side, as the church was undergoing repairs. Francisco went over there, between the baptismal font and the altar, and that was where I found him on my return.

Later, when he fell ill, he often told me, when I called in to see him on my way to school: "Look! Go to the church and give my love to the Hidden Jesus. What hurts me most is that

I cannot go there myself and stay awhile with the Hidden Jesus."

When I arrived at his house one day, I said goodbye to a group of school children who had come with me, and I went in to pay a visit to him and his sister. As he had heard all the noise, he asked me:

"Did you come with all that crowd?"

"Yes, I did."

"Don't go with them, because you might learn to commit sins. When you come out of school, go and stay for a little while near the Hidden Jesus, and afterwards come home by yourself."

On one occasion, I asked him:

"Francisco, do you feel very sick?"

"I do, but I'm suffering to console Our Lord."

When Jacinta and I went into his room one day, he said to us:

"Don't talk much today, as my head aches so badly."

"Don't forget to make the offering for sinners," Jacinta reminded him.

"Yes. But first I make it to console Our Lord and Our Lady, and then, afterwards, for sinners and for the Holy Father."

On another occasion, I found him very happy when I arrived.

"Are you better?"

"No. I feel worse. It won't be long now till I go to Heaven. When I'm there, I'm going to console Our Lord and Our Lady very much. Jacinta is going to pray a lot for sinners, for the Holy Father and for you. You will stay here, because Our Lady wants it that way. Listen, you must do everything that she tells you."

While Jacinta seemed to be solely concerned with the one thought of converting sinners and saving souls from going to Hell, Francisco appeared to think only of consoling Our Lady, who had seemed to him to be so sad.

FRANCISCO SEES THE DEVIL

How different is the incident that I now call to mind. One day we went to a place called Pedreira, and while the sheep were browsing, we jumped from rock to rock, making our voices echo down in the deep ravines. Francisco withdrew, as was his wont, to a hollow among the rocks.

A considerable time had elapsed, when we heard him shouting and crying out to us and to Our Lady. Distressed lest something might have happened to him, we ran in search of him, calling out his name.

"Where are you?"

"Here! Here!"

But it still took us some time before we could locate him. At last, we came upon him, trembling with fright, still on his knees, and so upset that he was unable to rise to his feet.

"What's wrong? What happened to you?"

In a voice half smothered with fright, he replied:

"It was one of those huge beasts that we saw in Hell. He was right here breathing out flames!"

I saw nothing, neither did Jacinta, so I laughed and said to him:

"You never want to think about Hell, so as not to be afraid; and now you're the first one to be frightened!"

Indeed, whenever Jacinta appeared particularly moved by the remembrance of Hell, he used to say to her:

"Don't think so much about Hell! Think about Our Lord and Our Lady instead. I don't think about Hell, so as not to be afraid."

He was anything but fearful. He'd go anywhere in the dark alone at night, without the slightest hesitation. He played with lizards, and when he came across any snakes, he got them to entwine themselves round a stick and even poured sheep's milk into the holes in the rocks for them to drink. He went hunting for foxes' holes and rabbits' burrows, for genets, and other creatures of the wilds.

FRANCISCO AND HIS FEATHERED FRIENDS

Francisco was very fond of birds and could not bear to see anyone robbing their nests. He always kept part of the bread he had for his lunch, breaking it into crumbs and spreading them out on top of the rocks, so that the birds could eat them. Moving away a little, he called them, as though he expected them to understand him. He didn't want anyone else to approach, lest they be frightened.

"Poor wee things! You are hungry," he said, as though conversing with them. "Come, come and eat!"

And they, keen-eyed as they are, did not wait for the invitation, but came flocking around him. It was his delight to see them flying back to the tree tops with their little craws full, singing and chirping in a deafening chorus, in which Francisco joined with rare skill.

One day we met a little boy carrying in his hand a small bird that he had caught. Full of compassion, Francisco promised him two coins if only he would let the bird fly away. The boy readily agreed. But first he wished to see the money in his hand. Francisco ran all the way home from the Carreira pond, which lies a little distance below the Cova da Iria, to fetch the coins, and so let the little prisoner free. Then, as he watched it fly away, he clapped his hands for joy and said: "Be careful! Don't let yourself be caught again."

Thereabouts, lived an old woman called Ti Maria Carreira, whose sons sent her out sometimes to take care of their flock of goats and sheep. The animals were rather wild and often strayed away in different directions. Whenever we met Ti Maria in these straits, Francisco was the first to run to her aid. He helped her to lead the flock to pasture, chased after the stray ones and gathered them all together again. The poor old woman overwhelmed Francisco with her thanks and called him her dear guardian angel.

When we came across any sick people, he was filled with compassion and said: "I can't bear to see them, as I feel so sorry for them! Tell them I'll pray for them."

One day, they wanted to take us to Montelo to the home of a man called Joaquim Chapeleta. Francisco did not want to go. "I'm not going, because I can't bear to see people who want to speak and cannot." (This man's mother was dumb).

When Jacinta and I returned home at nightfall, I asked my aunt where Francisco was.

"How do I know!" she replied. "I'm worn out looking for him all afternoon. Some ladies came and wanted to see you. But you two were not here. He vanished and never appeared again. Now you go and look for him!"

We sat down for a bit on a bench in the kitchen, thinking that we would go later to the Loca do Cabeço, certain that we would find him there. But no sooner had my aunt left the house, than his voice came from the attic through a little hole in the ceiling. He had climbed up there when he thought that some people were coming. From this vantage point he had observed everything that happened and told us afterwards:

"There were so many people! Heaven help me if they had ever caught me by myself! What ever would I have said to them?"

(There was a trap-door in the kitchen, which was easily reached by placing a chair on a table, thus affording access to the attic.)

FRANCISCO'S LOVE AND ZEAL

As I have already said, my aunt sold her flock before my mother disposed of ours. From then onwards, before I went out in the morning, I let Jacinta and Francisco know the place where I was going to pasture the sheep that day; as soon as they could get away, they came to join me.

One day, they were waiting for me when I arrived.

"Oh! How did you get here so early?"

"I came," answered Francisco, "because—I don't know why—being with you didn't matter much to me before, and I just came because of Jacinta; but now, I can't sleep in the morning, as I'm so anxious to be with you."

Once the Apparitions on each 13th of the month were over, he said to us on the eve of every following 13th:

"Look! Early tomorrow morning, I'm making my escape out through the back garden to the cave on the Cabeço. As soon as you can, come and join me there."

Oh dear! There I was, writing things about

31

his being sick and near to death, and now I see that I have gone back to the happy times we had on the serra, with the birds chirping merrily all around us. I ask your forgiveness. In writing down what I can remember, I am like a crab that walks backwards and forwards without bothering about reaching the end of its journey. I leave my work to Dr. Galamba, in case he can make use of anything in it, though I suppose he will find little or nothing.

I return, therefore, to Francisco's illness. But first, I will tell you something about his brief schooling. He came out of the house one day and met me with my sister Teresa, who was already married and living in Lomba. Another woman from a nearby hamlet had asked her to come to me about her son who had been accused of some crime which I no longer remember, and if he could not prove his innocence he was to be condemned, either to exile or to a term of some years imprisonment. Teresa asked me insistently, in the name of the poor woman for whom she wished to do such a favor, to plead for this grace with Our Lady. Having received the message, I set out for school, and on the way, I told my cousins all about it. When we reached Fatima, Francisco said to me:

"Listen! While you go to school, I'll stay with the Hidden Jesus, and I'll ask Him for that grace."

When I came out of school, I went to call him and asked:

"Did you pray to Our Lord to grant that grace?"

"Yes, I did. Tell your Teresa that he'll be home in a few days' time."

And indeed, a few days later, the poor boy returned home. On the 13th, he and his entire family came to thank Our Lady for the grace they had received.

On another occasion I noticed, as we left the house, that Francisco was walking very slowly:

"What's the matter?" I asked him. "You seem unable to walk!"

"I've such a bad headache, and I feel as though I'm going to fall."

"Then don't come. Stay at home!"

"I don't want to. I'd rather stay in the church with the Hidden Jesus, while you go to school."

Francisco was already sick, but could still manage to walk a little, so one day I went with him to the cave on the Cabeço and to Valinhos. On our return home, we found the house full of people. A poor woman was standing near a table, pretending to bless innumerable pious objects: rosary beads, medals, crucifixes and so on. Jacinta and I were soon surrounded by a crowd of people who wanted to question us. Francisco was seized upon by the would-be "blesser," who invited him to help her.

"I could not give a blessing," he replied very

33

seriously, "and neither should you! Only priests do that."

The little boy's words went round the crowd like lightning, as though spoken by some loudspeaker, and the poor woman had to make a quick departure amid a hail of insults from the people, all demanding back the objects they had just handed over to her.

I already related in my account of Jacinta, how he managed to go one day to the Cova da Iria; how he wore the rope and then handed it back to me; how he was the first, on a day when the heat was suffocating, to offer the sacrifice of not taking a drink; and how he sometimes reminded his sister about suffering for sinners, and so on. I presume, therefore, that it is not necessary to repeat these things here.

One day, I was by his bedside, keeping him company. Jacinta, who had gotten up for a while, was there too. Suddenly, his sister Teresa came to warn us that a veritable multitude of people were coming down the road and were obviously looking for us. As soon as she had gone out, I said to Francisco: "All right! You two wait for them here. I'm going to hide."

Jacinta managed to run out behind me, and we both succeeded in concealing ourselves inside a barrel which was overturned just outside the door leading to the back garden. It was not long before we heard the noise of people searching the house, going out through the garden and even standing right beside the barrel; but we were saved by the fact that its open end was turned in the opposite direction.

When we felt that they had all gone away, we came out of our hiding place and went to rejoin Francisco, who told us all that had happened.

"There were so many people, and they wanted me to tell them where you were, but I didn't know myself. They wished to see us and ask us lots of things. Besides that, there was a woman from Alqueidão, who wanted the cure of a sick person and the conversion of a sinner. I'll pray for that woman, and you pray for the others—there's such a lot of them."

Shortly after Francisco's death, this woman came to see us, and asked me to show her his grave. She wished to go there and thank him for the two graces for which she had asked him to pray.

One day, we were just outside Aljustrel, on our way to the Cova da Iria, when a group of people came upon us by surprise around the bend in the road. In order the better to see and hear us, they set Jacinta and myself on top of a wall. Francisco refused to let himself be put there, as though he were afraid of falling. Then, little by little, he edged his way out and leaned against a dilapidated wall on the opposite side. A poor woman and her son, seeing that they could not manage to speak to us personally, as they wished, went and knelt down in front of Francisco. They begged him to obtain from Our Lady the grace that the father of the family would be cured and that he would not have to go to the war. Francisco knelt down also, took off his cap and asked if they would like to pray the Rosary with him. They said they would, and began to pray. Very soon, all those people stopped asking curious questions and also went down on their knees to pray. After that, they went with us to the Cova da Iria, reciting a Rosary along the way. Once there, we said another Rosary, and then they went away, quite happy.

The poor woman promised to come back and thank Our Lady for the graces she had asked for, if they were granted. She came back several times, accompanied not only by her son but also her husband, who had by now recovered. They came from the parish of S. Mamede, and we called them the Casaleiros.

FRANCISCO'S ILLNESS

While he was ill, Francisco always appeared joyful and content. I asked him sometimes:

"Are you suffering a lot, Francisco?"

"Quite a lot, but never mind! I am suffering to console Our Lord, and afterwards, within a short time, I am going to Heaven!"

"Once you get there, don't forget to ask Our Lady to take me there soon as well."

"That, I won't ask! You know very well that she doesn't want you there yet."

The day before he died, he said to me:

"Look! I am very ill; it won't be long now before I go to Heaven."

"Then listen to this. When you're there, don't forget to pray a great deal for sinners, for the Holy Father, for me and for Jacinta."

"Yes, I'll pray. But look, you'd better ask Jacinta to pray for these things instead, because I'm afraid I'll forget when I see Our Lord. And then, more than anything else I want to console Him."

One day, early in the morning, his sister Teresa came looking for me.

"Come quickly to our house! Francisco is very bad and says he wants to tell you something."

I dressed as fast as I could and went over there. He asked his mother and brothers and sisters to leave the room, saying that he wanted to ask me a secret. They went out, and he said to me:

"I am going to confession so that I can receive Holy Communion and then die. I want you to tell me if you have seen me commit any sin, and then go and ask Jacinta if she has seen me commit any."

"You disobeyed your mother a few times," I answered, "when she told you to stay at home, and you ran off to be with me or to go and hide."

"That's true. I remember that. Now go and

ask Jacinta if she remembers anything else."

I went, and Jacinta thought for a while, then answered:

"Well, tell him that, before Our Lady appeared to us, he stole a coin from our father to buy a music box from José Marto of Casa Velha; and when the boys from Aljustrel threw stones at those from Boleiros, he threw some too!"

When I gave him this message from his sister, he answered:

"I've already confessed those, but I'll do so again. Maybe, it is because of these sins that I committed that Our Lord is so sad! But even if I don't die, I'll never commit them again. I'm heartily sorry for them now." Joining his hands, he recited the prayer: "O my Jesus, forgive us, save us from the fire of Hell, lead all souls to Heaven, especially those who are most in need."

Then he said: "Now listen, you must also ask Our Lord to forgive me my sins."

"I'll ask that, don't worry. If Our Lord had not forgiven them already, Our Lady would not have told Jacinta the other day that she was coming soon to take you to Heaven. Now, I'm going to Mass, and there I'll pray to the Hidden Jesus for you."

"Then, please ask Him to let the parish priest give me Holy Communion."

"I certainly will."

When I returned from the church, Jacinta

had already gotten up and was sitting on his bed. As soon as Francisco saw me, he asked:

"Did you ask the Hidden Jesus that the parish priest would give me Holy Communion?"

"I did."

"Then, in Heaven, I'll pray for you."

"You will? The other day, you said you wouldn't!"

"That was about taking you there very soon. But if you want me to pray for that, I will, and then let Our Lady do as she wishes."

"Yes, do. You pray."

"All right. Don't worry, I'll pray."

Then I left them and went off to my usual daily tasks of lessons and work. When I came home at night, I found him radiant with joy. He had made his confession, and the parish priest had promised to bring him Holy Communion next day.

On the following day, after receiving Holy Communion, he said to his sister:

"I am happier than you are, because I have the Hidden Jesus within my heart. I'm going to Heaven, but I'm going to pray very much to Our Lady for them to bring you both there soon."

Jacinta and I spent almost the whole of that day at his bedside. As he was already unable to pray, he asked us to pray the Rosary for him. Then he said to me:

"I am sure I shall miss you terribly in

Heaven. If only Our Lady would bring you there soon, also!"

"You won't miss me! Just imagine! And you right there with Our Lord and Our Lady! They are so good!"

"That's true! Perhaps I won't remember!"

Then I added: "Perhaps you'll forget! But never mind!"

FRANCISCO'S HOLY DEATH

That night I said goodbye to him.

"Goodbye, Francisco! If you go to Heaven tonight, don't forget me when you get there, do you hear me?"

"No, I won't forget. Be sure of that." Then, seizing my right hand, he held it tightly for a long time, looking at me with tears in his eyes.

"Do you want anything more?" I asked him, with tears running down my cheeks too.

"No!" he answered in a low voice, quite overcome.

As the scene was becoming so moving, my aunt told me to leave the room.

"Goodbye then, Francisco! Till we meet in Heaven, goodbye!..."

Heaven was drawing near. He took his flight to Heaven the following day in the arms of his heavenly Mother. I could never describe how much I missed him. This grief was a thorn that pierced my heart for years to come. It is a memory of the past that echoes forever unto eternity.

Verification of the mortal remains of Ven. Francisco Marto of Fatima. The author states he has it on good authority that when the verification of the mortal remains of Ven. Francisco Marto took place on March 13, 1952, the rosary that had been placed in his hand when he was put into the coffin was found imbedded in his fingers.

PRAYER FOR THE BEATIFICATION
OF FRANCISCO MARTO OF FATIMA
(For private recitation)

God has already granted many graces through his intercession. The preparatory canonical process for his beatification began in 1949.

MOST Holy Trinity, Father, Son and Holy Ghost, I adore Thee profoundly with all the powers of my soul, and I thank Thee for the apparitions of the Most Holy Virgin in Fatima, which have made manifest to the world the treasures of her Immaculate Heart.

By the infinite merits of the Sacred Heart of Jesus and through the intercession of the Immaculate Heart of Mary, I implore Thee—if it should be for Thy greater glory and the good of our souls—to glorify in the sight of Thy Holy Church Francisco, the shepherd of Fatima, granting us through his intercession the grace which we implore. Amen.

IMPRIMATUR, Fatimae, 13 Octobris 1960
† JOANNES, Episcopus Leiriensis

PRAYER FOR THE BEATIFICATION
OF JACINTA MARTO OF FATIMA
(For private recitation)

God has already given many extraordinary graces through her intercession. The Process for the Beatification of the Servant of God, Jacinta Marto, was sent to the Sacred Congregation in Rome on the 2nd of July, 1979.

MOST Holy Trinity, Father, Son and Holy Ghost, I adore Thee profoundly with all the powers of my soul, and I thank Thee for the apparitions of the Most Holy Virgin in Fatima, which have made manifest to the world the treasures of her Immaculate Heart.

By the infinite merits of the Sacred Heart of Jesus and through the intercession of the Immaculate Heart of Mary, I implore Thee—if it should be for Thy greater glory and the good of our souls—to glorify in the sight of Thy Holy Church Jacinta, the shepherdess of Fatima, granting us through her intercession the grace which we implore. Amen.

Our Father, Hail Mary, Glory be to the Father.

Please send details of any favors received through the intercession of Jacinta Marto to the following address: Vice-Postulador da Causa de Jacinta Marto, Apartado 6, P-2496 FATIMA, Codex Portugal.

IMPRIMATUR, Leiren, 20 Februarii 1980
† ALBERTUS, Episcopus Leiriensis

Fatima, The Rosary, the Sacred Heart...

6 CRUCIAL BOOKLETS
by Msgr. Jos. A. Cirrincione

1185 VEN. JACINTA MARTO OF FATIMA. Msgr. Jos. A. Cirrincione. Dead at only 10, Ven. Jacinta, after the Fatima apparitions, had dedicated her life to perpetual reparation for the conversion of sinners and thus gained great sanctity. Here is her remarkable story! (5—.80 ea.; 10—.70 ea.; 25—.60 ea.; 100—.50 ea.; 500—.40 ea.; 1,000—.35 ea.). (ISBN-4801). 100,000 Sold! **1.50**

1125 FATIMA'S MESSAGE FOR OUR TIMES. Msgr. Jos. A. Cirrincione. Fatima has been called "a summary of the Gospels." Summarizes the Fatima messages as a return to a life of prayer, to the traditional prayer life of the Catholic Church, especially to prayer before the Blessed Sacrament. Great on the value of Holy Hours—a forgotten spiritual weapon. (5—.80 ea.; 10—.70 ea.; 25—.60 ea.; 100—.50 ea.; 500—.40 ea.; 1,000—.35 ea.). (ISBN-4038). 100,000 Sold! **1.50**

0213 FORGOTTEN SECRET OF FATIMA. Msgr. Jos. A. Cirrincione. Refocuses our attention on the overriding (but now for the most part "forgotten") message of Fatima: *"Many souls go to Hell because there are none to sacrifice themselves and pray for them."* Offers an easy method to fulfill Our Lady's request and live the message in a completely practical way. Challenging! (5—.80 ea.; 10—.70 ea.; 25—.60 ea.; 50—.50 ea.; 100—.45 ea.; 500—.40 ea.; 1,000—.35 ea.). (ISBN-3376). 90,000 Sold! **1.25**

1070 SAINT JOSEPH, FATIMA AND FATHER-HOOD. Msgr. Jos. A. Cirrincione. On October 13, 1917, before the "Miracle of the Sun," St. Joseph appeared holding the Child Jesus; both were blessing the world. Draws some profound and sobering conclusions—both for the Church and for the world! (5—.70 ea.; 10—.60 ea.; 25—.50 ea.; 100—.45 ea.; 500—.40 ea.; 1,000—.35 ea.). (ISBN-3848). 175,000 Sold! **1.25**

1040 THE ROSARY AND THE CRISIS OF FAITH—Fatima and World Peace. Msgr. Jos. A. Cirrincione. How the Rosary will lead to the triumph of the Immaculate Heart of Mary in our present crisis of Faith. Great 3-page summary of the entire Fatima message. Surprising and excellent. (5—.60 ea.; 10—.55 ea.; 25—.50 ea.; 50—.45 ea.; 100—.40 ea.; 500—.35 ea.; 1,000—.30 ea.). (ISBN-3066). 600,000 Sold! **1.25**

1026 I WAIT FOR YOU—Jesus' Lament over Man's Indifference. Msgr. Jos. A. Cirrincione. Jesus' own powerful words from *The Way of Divine Love* showing His displeasure over mankind's neglect of His love, especially of His Eucharistic presence. One can easily read this booklet 2 or 3 times. The impact is terrific! (5—.50 ea.; 10—.45 ea.; 25—.40 ea.; 50—.35 ea.; 100—.30 ea.; 500—.25 ea.; 1,000—.20 ea.). (ISBN-285X). 500,000 Sold! **.75**

At your local bookstore or direct from the publisher!

TAN BOOKS AND PUBLISHERS, INC.
P.O. Box 424, Rockford, Illinois 61105

If you have enjoyed this book, consider making your next selection from among the following . . .

The Forgotten Secret of Fatima...................... 1.25
Characters of the Inquisition. *Walsh*.................12.50
Teilhardism and the New Religion. *Smith*...........12.00
The Facts about Luther. *O'Hare*.....................13.50
Pope St. Pius X. *F.A. Forbes*.......................... 6.00
St. Alphonsus Liguori. *Miller & Aubin*...............15.00
St. Teresa of Avila. *Walsh*...........................18.00
Therese Neumann—Mystic and Stigmatist. *Vogl*......11.00
Life of the Blessed Virgin Mary. *Emmerich*.........15.00
The Way of Divine Love. (pocket, unabr.) *Sr. Menendez* 8.50
Light and Peace. *Quadrupani*......................... 5.00
Where We Got the Bible. *Graham*..................... 5.00
St. Catherine of Siena. *Curtayne*....................12.00
Trustful Surrender to Divine Providence............. 4.00
Charity for the Suffering Souls. *Nageleisen*..........15.00
The Voice of the Saints. (Sayings of)................ 5.00
Catholic Apologetics. *Laux*.......................... 8.00
St. Rose of Lima. *Sr. Alphonsus*....................12.50
The Devil—Does He Exist? *Delaporte*.............. 5.00
A Catechism of Modernism. *Lemius*................. 4.00
St. Bernadette Soubirous. *Trochu*...................16.50
The Love of Mary. *Roberto*......................... 7.00
A Prayerbook of Favorite Litanies. *Hebert*.......... 9.00
The 12 Steps to Holiness and Salvation. *Liguori*...... 7.00
The Rosary and the Crisis of Faith................. 1.25
Child's Bible History. *Knecht*...................... 4.00
St. Pius V. *Anderson*............................... 4.00
St. Joan of Arc. *Beevers*........................... 8.00
Eucharistic Miracles. *Cruz*.........................13.00
The Blessed Virgin Mary. *St. Alphonsus*............ 4.50
The Priesthood. *Stockums*...........................11.00
Soul of the Apostolate. *Chautard*................... 9.00
Little Catechism of the Curé of Ars. *St. J. Vianney*... 5.50
The Four Last Things. *von Cochem*................. 5.00
The Curé of Ars. *O'Brien*.......................... 4.50
Beyond Space—A Book about the Angels. *Parente*.... 7.00

Prices guaranteed through December 31, 1995.

Prices guaranteed through December 31, 1995.

Prices guaranteed through December 31, 1995.